sonder.

The realisation that each passerby is living a life as vivid and complex as your own, filled with their own ambitions, fears, routines, and memories, all quietly unfolding alongside yours.

OrangeBooks Publication

1st Floor, Rajhans Arcade, Mall Road, Kohka, Bhilai, Chhattisgarh 490020

Website: **www.orangebooks.in**

First Edition, 2025

ISBN: 978-93-7426-962-6

Price: Rs. 299.00

Printed in India

sonder.

Khyati Singh

OrangeBooks Publication
www.orangebooks.in

this isn't deep (but maybe it should've been)

I've always said, "it's not that deep."

It's my default response to anything and everything going on around me—a soft exit from conversations I don't want to finish, a loophole out of vulnerability.

It works, most of the time.

But some things don't leave when you tell them to. A sentence someone said without thinking.

The silence after a message I never sent.

A stranger I locked eyes with for two seconds and never saw again.

Moments so minor they shouldn't exist. But they do, in the back of my mind, like tabs I forgot to close.

This book is made of those.

The ones that looked like nothing. That felt like background noise. That happened, and then never quite unhappened.

Most of it is just small stuff. Micro-interactions. Missed signals. Emotional buffering.

The people I drifted from. The people I stalked but never texted. The people I became and stopped being.

Sometimes it's about other people. Sometimes it's about the versions of myself I quietly offloaded when no one was watching.

No big narrative. No resolution.

Just quiet exits. Pattern recognition. A timeline of glitches and soft reboots.

We watch shows where the main characters' life moves in perfect arcs. But real life doesn't cast anyone in the lead.

And I know I'm not the first person to say that, it's not some mind-blowing realisation I came up with in the shower.

But it's still worth repeating.

Because the second we forget that, we start living for an audience that doesn't exist. We obsess over how we're seen instead of just being. We turn ourselves into content.

I’m not the main character in most of these moments. Sometimes I’m the background noise.

Sometimes I’m the one remembering someone who doesn’t remember me.

And if none of this hits? That’s okay. You’ll forget it.

But if one thing sticks, a line, a memory, a face you didn’t mean to think about, maybe that’s enough.

You don’t have to remember the whole book. Just one moment.

Just one person you thought you’d forgotten.

So no, this isn’t deep.

But if it makes you feel something anyway then maybe we both just lied a little.

contents

the smile economy

Every morning around 7:10, I'd walk to the school bus stop, half-awake, uniform creased, earphones in but not playing anything. The path was mostly quiet, but never empty. Always the same cast of people. Like an unspoken routine we'd all signed up for.

One woman was always on a call, not casual catching up, but full-throttle negotiations with someone on the other end of her Bluetooth, like something urgent couldn't wait until business hours.

Another walked her golden retriever. Sometimes she was alone. At other times, her daughter, probably seven years old, would tag along, stepping into puddles on purpose.

Two men, maybe around my grandfather's age, walked side by side in total sync. They had the kind of smiles that didn't feel performative; they just *were*.

And then there was one woman with kind eyes, whom I didn't smile at for weeks. I don't know why. Some instinctive deflection. But when I finally did, she smiled back in a way that felt like I should've done it sooner.

None of this was planned. None of it needed to happen. But eventually, it did. I started smiling at them, just a flicker, a nod, enough to be seen.

There was no reward. No cost. It was just something I started doing. And kept doing it.

In hindsight, those interactions were positive externalities in action, small individual behaviours that unintentionally create benefits for others. A smile doesn't take anything away from me. But it might soften someone's morning, even if I never find out. In economic theory, that's value created *outside* a transaction. No one's paying for it. No one's tracking it. But it shifts the experience of a moment just slightly enough to matter.

What makes a positive externality powerful is its scale: one person smiling doesn't change much. However, if dozens do it every morning across a city, it subtly transforms the public space's mood. The aggregate effect becomes part of the emotional infrastructure.

More interesting, though, is how the system stayed stable without a formal incentive. In microeconomics, most human interactions are modelled on utility maximisation, doing things that benefit us directly. But smiling doesn't fit cleanly into that. It's too small, too uncertain. It only makes sense if you start including *non-monetary utility*, psychological ease, a sense of rhythm, and the emotional payoff of being part of a pattern.

If I look at it through a computer science lens, the whole thing functioned like a lightweight network protocol, designed not for major data transfer, but just to confirm a connection. In distributed systems, we use heartbeat signals, small, recurring pings between devices to say, "I'm here. Still running. Still okay." The smile was that. A social heartbeat.

There was no deeper data attached. No message. That's called stateless communication, where each interaction exists independently, without needing memory of the last one. But when repeated, it creates expectation. Over time, the smile becomes a cached behaviour, a stored routine that others recognise and respond to. That's caching: storing prior outputs to speed up future responses.

And if the behaviour breaks, if I stop smiling, the system doesn't crash. But it degrades. The walk feels colder. I feel more invisible. Systems don't always fail loudly.

Sometimes they just lose warmth, efficiency, and human texture.

Eventually, I stopped taking that route. New schedule. New bus stop. I didn't say goodbye; it didn't feel like the kind of thing that needed a goodbye. But part of me still wonders if someone noticed.

Maybe one of the men turned his head one morning, just slightly. Maybe the woman with kind eyes kept smiling at the empty space. Or maybe, just as likely, the system adapted. It always does.

What I learned from that season of my life is this:

You don't need deep relationships to make a system meaningful. You need consistent, low-friction participation.

A smile. A nod. A recognition loop.

What economists call non-excludable and non-rivalrous goods, things everyone can access and share at the same time without diminishing their value.

This is how cities stay human.

Not through policy or infrastructure, but through tiny, untracked moments of empathy, emotional surplus, built quietly, passed forward invisibly.

I didn’t smile at them because I was kind. I smiled because I could.

And somehow, that was enough to keep the system running.

That’s the economy. That’s the code.

people in traffic

Being in traffic is like watching someone's life behind glass. You don't know them, but for a few seconds, your timelines align, same road, same weather, same traffic, and then you diverge.

A woman applying lipstick at a red light. A man speaking into his Bluetooth headset as if something's already gone wrong. A kid in the backseat, forehead against the window, aged into stillness.

And once, a man who looked like he was crying. Or maybe not. Maybe just frozen. Hands on the wheel, radio off, expression unreadable. The kind of stillness that could mean anything, grief, exhaustion, or nothing at all.

Then the light changed. And he disappeared.

Every car around you is a sealed-off decision tree in motion. Not random, just invisible. Each route, each pause, each risky merge is the output of a private algorithm: speed vs. safety, silence vs. contact, peace vs. urgency.

You don't just pass strangers.

You pass their opportunity structures, the invisible scaffolding of what they weighed, what they dropped, and what they never even realised they gave up.

Opportunity cost is the value of the next best thing you didn't choose.

Most of these losses are quiet: a longer route that might've felt better, a call left undialed, a small detour that could've saved their whole morning.

And the eerie part is that many of them don't even know what they gave up, because decisions made at the margin barely register.

In marginal utility theory, what we choose isn't about big leaps; it's about the *next* unit of ease, the next second saved.

That's what you're watching: thousands of tiny optimisations that seldom look like choices at all

The system should fail.

But it doesn't, because it's built to handle delay.

Real-time systems operate without perfect information or perfect timing. There is no master clock. Inputs arrive late. Outputs lag.

The delay between input and action is called latency, and in traffic, it's baked into everything.

You're reacting not to what's happening, but to what already happened, two seconds ago, outside your line of sight.

Everyone's running asynchronously. No one's caught up.

But we all pretend like we are.

Somehow, it still holds.

Not because it's efficient, but because it's forgiving.

Distributed systems survive through redundancy and slack. You wait an extra beat. You don't honk. You leave space for someone to fail safely.

No one formalised this. But the system would break without it.

Each of us becomes a node in the larger network, passing imperfect signals down the line. Sometimes they misfire.

Sometimes they ripple too far.

But most of the time, they land well enough.

Where they're going. Who they're thinking about. What they just left behind. You won't know.

But sometimes, like with that man at the red light, you remember.

What if he wasn't crying? What if I was wrong?

What mattered more, the truth, or the fact that I noticed at all?

We simulate lives we'll never debug, stitching sense from incomplete code. That's why traffic feels harder than it should.

Not because you're stuck.

Because you're surrounded by people, guessing, reacting, just barely making it work.

There's no narrator here.

No one's logging your efforts. You calculate. You adapt.

No one claps.

You're just another node in a laggy, fault-tolerant network Trying to arrive.

Trying not to crash on the way there.

if i were my brother

One day at lunch, a friend asked, almost casually:

"If you could switch lives with anyone, who would it be?"

Someone said Elon Musk. Another said Bella Hadid.

The usual, people reaching outward, upward, anywhere but here.

And then she said, quietly: "My brother."

The table went silent. No one followed.

It wasn't the kind of answer that invited a joke or a follow-up.

And though we never spoke about it again, the stillness of that moment lingered.

At first, I thought she meant it in passing, something sentimental.

But the more I thought about it, the more I realised what she had really said: She didn't want to be *someone else*.

She wanted to stay within the orbit of the life she already loved.

There was something deeply human in that, this quiet resistance to change.

In computer science, systems naturally resist abrupt change; they stabilise around what's known as equilibrium states.

Too much input too fast, and the system crashes.

Humans are built the same way.

We cling to the familiar because it keeps us coherent. It's not complacency, it's preservation.

Her brother wasn't an escape; he was a constant.

She didn't want fame, or reinvention, or an entirely new simulation.

She just wanted to live within the small, stable loop she understood, where breakfast tasted the same, the light hit the same kitchen tiles, and laughter came from familiar voices.

In economics, we'd call that understanding the opportunity cost, recognising that choosing one life means giving up infinite others.

But she seemed okay with that.

She had made peace with her trade-offs.

And in doing so, she reminded me that equilibrium, the balance between what we desire and what we have, isn't failure.

It's grace.

We never spoke about that lunch again.

The trays clattered, the bell rang, and we went back to our classes, the simulation quietly resetting.

But her answer stayed lodged somewhere in my head like code that refuses to compile until you understand what it means.

I think about how sonder, the realisation that everyone lives a life as vivid and layered as your own, sometimes also means realising that some people don't want expansion.

They just want stillness.

A stable loop.

A code that runs without interference.

In that moment, she made me grateful for the systems I live within—the family dinners, the small conversations, the messy yet predictable variables that make my life mine.

Her resistance to change wasn't a limitation; it was an act of gratitude. A soft reminder that not every update is an improvement.

Some are just noise.

And maybe that's what makes us human. We don't always seek optimisation.

Sometimes, we just want continuity.

To run our existing code a little longer, without crashing.

She didn't want to trade lives.

She wanted to stay where she already belonged.

And maybe, that's the rarest kind of contentment there is.

digital surveillance, but make it soft

You stalk people you'll never message. You tell yourself it's curiosity, or maybe boredom, but it's closer to maintenance, the digital equivalent of checking if a plant is still alive. You scroll, you tap, you pause longer on some faces than others.

You think you're invisible, but you're not. You're just another entry in the system logs, one more observer pretending detachment is neutrality. Every second of attention becomes a quiet vote, a microtransaction.

There's a strange economy to this kind of looking. Value no longer comes from what you make, but from how long someone looks. You start monitoring your own presence like a fluctuating currency, tracking impressions, reach, and the invisible metrics of being seen. Too much visibility feels expensive; too little feels like depreciation. Even silence has a cost in this market.

And then, sometimes, the algorithm isn't digital at all.

On my way home one evening, in an autorickshaw, the driver asked for a little extra at the end of the ride. Not aggressively, just a quiet request wrapped in exhaustion. I said yes, and he nodded, eyes still on the road.

The whole ride back, I kept thinking about him. What his day looked like, what time he woke up, and what his evening might be. Whether he drove all night. Whether he had kids waiting for him. Whether he thought about the people who sat in the backseat, half-lost in their own worlds.

It struck me how easily we build entire lives from fragments, how a few seconds of data become an entire model. You generate an entire distribution from a single data point. You guess, infer, and fill in the blanks until a person starts to look statistically complete.

That's what asymmetric information does: one side assumes, the other absorbs. Economists study it in markets; we live it every day. Every assumption becomes a small distortion, a bias you don't realise you're reinforcing.

Maybe that's what I was doing, caching a version of him. Saving an image to revisit later, like data stored in a place I'd never return to.

Memory as browser history.

Guilt disguised as data collection.

We do this constantly, online, offline, everywhere. Our minds work like browsers left open too long, tabs multiplying, history syncing between devices. We tell ourselves we're just observing, but really, we're archiving. We don't want to forget, not because we care deeply, but because forgetting feels like deleting proof that something once existed.

We've learned to look open while staying encrypted. We curate what others see while pretending we don't.

Maybe sonder, the quiet understanding that everyone else's life is as layered and chaotic as your own, is the last kind of privacy left. Not because it hides people, but because it restores them. It reminds you that not everything seen is meant to be known, and not every trace needs to be followed.

That autorickshaw driver probably doesn't remember me. But I still remember his voice, the way he said "madam" without looking back. I think about how often we occupy each other's peripheries, visible but unread.

Sonder asks you to pause there. To see without trying to decode.

To accept that every person's algorithm runs differently,
trained on data you'll never have access to.

And that's okay.

drift theory

A childhood friend you knew everything about. Now, nothing. No fallout. No betrayal. Just silence, delay, and drift.

At first, you both keep replying, slower, shorter, thinner, until one day, you stop expecting the notification. The friendship doesn't end. It just *expires quietly*, like a license that was never renewed.

That's what drift feels like, not the crash, but the soft un-syncing.

In code, there's something called a *deprecated function.* It still exists in the system, still callable, still technically functional, but no longer supported. It's there for legacy reasons. The system keeps it so that older programs don't break. But new updates never reach it. No more debugging. No more patching.

Sometimes, I think people are like that, too. Still stored in memory, no longer executed.

Drift happens slowly. It isn't dramatic; it's algorithmic.

Like feedback loops decaying over time, the input weakens, the signal fades, the connection thins until it's indistinguishable from noise.

You remember birthdays months late. You notice you've stopped sending links, stopped asking if they've heard that new song you love. One day, you scroll past their post without liking it, and it feels like crossing a line.

But there's no villain here. Just changing operating systems.

You updated. They didn't. Or maybe they did, and you were the one who didn't install the patch.

There's a reel I once saw, "I'm a mosaic of everyone I've ever loved."

I think that's true. I act like the people I've loved, friends, classmates, and even acquaintances. I pick up their phrases, their music, their gestures. I imitate without realising. Not because I want to copy them, but because that's how my system learns.

Maybe it's because I grew up alone. No sibling to mirror, no template to test identity against. So I learned by absorbing other people's traits, treating each person as a dataset, collecting bits of behaviour, running quiet simulations to see what fits.

Economists call this *path dependence*: the idea that your future options depend on the routes you've already taken. Once a behaviour or preference is reinforced enough, it becomes your default. You stop choosing, you start repeating.

That's what drift really is.

The unintentional consequence of optimisation.

You become efficient at letting go. You conserve emotional energy.

You adapt to silence as if it were equilibrium.

In economics, systems tend toward efficiency, but efficiency isn't the same as happiness. Frictionless communication sounds ideal until you realise friction was how you felt presence. The pauses, the misread messages, the awkward overlaps, they were proof that both sides were still trying to sync.

Now everything is seamless, and nothing feels alive.

The same goes for people. Drift isn't laziness; it's entropy.

A natural movement toward lower energy states, away from emotional intensity, toward comfortable distance.

You don't even notice it until the distance stabilises into a habit.

Sometimes, I scroll through old photos like they're obsolete code, lines written by a past version of myself, running on an operating system that no longer exists. I recognise the syntax, but I don't know how to execute it anymore.

That's the quiet cruelty of memory. It caches what you can't run again.

And yet, drift isn't always loss.

Maybe it's how the system preserves itself, deleting unnecessary background processes, freeing up bandwidth.

Sonder helps here. It reminds you that while you've been moving forward, so have they. Their code, too, has evolved. Their emotional architecture has been patched, debugged, and recompiled without you in the loop.

You're both still running, just on different servers now.

The connection isn't gone; it's just archived. Sometimes, stability looks like disconnection.

So when I think about that friend, the one I once knew everything about, I try not to feel guilt. I think of drift as maintenance. As graceful degradation. As the system learning how to survive updates without crashing.

Because people aren't programs. We don't deprecate, we repurpose.

Every person you've loved leaves a trace in your source code.

A function you might never call again, but that still shapes how everything else runs.

And maybe that's what makes sonder essential.

It reminds you that no one truly disappears; they just migrate to a different process, a different loop, a different life.

You can't access their system anymore, but you can still respect its design.

You can still remember that every drift was mutual, two algorithms diverging, each optimising for survival.

the self-view mirror

The screen lights up before it fully turns on. For half a second, the reflection flickers, too bright, too close, too raw. You stare. You tilt your head, fix your hair, smile once, twice. Delete. Try again. It's almost a ritual now, this small negotiation between who you think you are and who the lens insists on showing.

You look different in pictures than you do in mirrors. Everyone does. The mirror offers familiarity, your reflection filtered through muscle memory, the version you've quietly approved after years of glancing, adjusting, forgiving. But the camera? The camera is indifferent. It translates you into numbers and angles, the geometry of someone else's gaze. You never quite look like how you imagined.

It's strange how technology returns your face to you slightly altered, how your reflection begins to belong to everyone but you. The mirror tells you how you feel; the photo tells you how you appear. Between them is a small but constant dissonance. You start curating yourself in response, changing expressions, softening features, learning what "works." Somewhere along the way, the reflection stops reflecting and starts instructing.

I used to think mirrors were neutral, just light bouncing back. But they remember, in small ways. The bathroom mirror that fogs while you brush your teeth has seen every anxious morning. The one in your room knows the tilt of your posture when you're tired. Even shop windows, those accidental mirrors, catch you off guard, showing versions you don't recognise. Versions that don't perform.

There's something deeply modern about that, this constant toggling between images, each one demanding to be believed. You start becoming fluent in self-correction. Not because anyone asked you to, but because you've learned that reflection is a kind of reputation. You post, edit, wait for the soft approval of hearts and eyes. Each image becomes a tiny proof of existence.

But it's exhausting, too, to live at a distance from your own face. To know that even your reflection has an audience. Somewhere, you start wondering: what's truer? The version that feels right to you, or the one the camera insists on?

Once, while riding home after a long day, I caught my reflection in the rickshaw's rearview mirror. The glass was scratched, the light uneven. My face looked older, softer, somehow more honest. It wasn't pretty. But it was me, unposed, unfiltered, mid-thought. There was comfort in that unintentional clarity.

Maybe that's the quiet truth of growing up in a mirrored world: learning to live with multiple selves. The one you recognise. The one you share. The one you can't control. Each reflection teaches you how others might see you, a slow education in empathy. Because everyone is carrying their own distortion, their own lighting, their own unflattering angle.

And maybe sonder begins there, in the realisation that perception is never stable. That is the way you appear to others is as fragile, as flickering, as the way they appear to you. We're all just reflections trying to find the right distance from the light.

Sometimes, when I open the front camera by accident, I still flinch. The image loads with that split-second delay, unready, imperfect. But lately, I've stopped retaking. I let the photo stay, grainy and badly lit. It's not symmetrical, not flattering, not optimised. But it's mine.

And maybe that's what it means to be seen: not perfectly, but fully, even when the mirror lies, even when the camera corrects, even when you no longer know which version is closest to the truth.

how to disappear (without saying goodbye)

It starts small. A delayed reply, a half-hearted smile, a conversation cut short. You don't announce the departure. You just thin yourself out. You lower the frequency of your presence, like a signal fading into static.

Sometimes it's literal: skipping a gathering, taking a different route home, declining a message. Sometimes it's emotional, letting yourself drift from people whose rhythm no longer matches yours. There's no anger, no rupture, just a slow erosion of proximity.

I remember scrolling past a message I wanted to reply to desperately, my fingers hovering over the screen, itching to tell them everything, every laugh, every annoyance, every small victory of my day. My biggest fear has always been losing the people I love, even if it's just losing touch. I'm terrible at letting go. I cling. I want them all to myself. But I've been learning, imperfectly, that you can't make someone stay if they don't want to.

Everyone has their own intricate lives, as vivid and detailed as mine.

The people who once filled entire afternoons of my life, friends who knew my every joke, every pause, every hesitation, now flicker past in my feed. Faces that once demanded attention now pass like minor variables in a system I no longer operate within. No fallouts. No fights. Just silence. Just drift.

Sometimes I remember the moments that are gone forever: the last time I hugged a friend, or held hands with someone whose warmth I thought would last. I remember the sound of their laughter in the hallway, the exact pause before they answered a joke only I would make. And then, suddenly, I don't know anything about them anymore. I don't know how they go about their day, what they eat for breakfast, what worries make their heart tighten. The richness of their life, the lives I used to see so clearly, has become a parallel universe I can glimpse only in fragments.

And yet, in that drift, there's a soft intelligence. You learn which presences need tending and which can survive absence. You measure emotional costs unconsciously: how much do I give, how much do I take, how much can I step back before the connection fractures entirely? You vanish without friction because you've realised confrontation is expensive, and sometimes letting go softly is a form of care.

There's a certain poetry in that. A quiet understanding that people are not static. They move, just as you do, and sometimes the best way to maintain balance is to recede. To become a background process in someone else's life, barely noticed, quietly stabilising the system.

One evening, the screen glowed too brightly in the dark room. I caught myself smiling at an old message I never sent, a fragment of someone else's world, suspended in time. My fingers hovered over the keyboard, lingering over words I no longer needed to write. I didn't answer. I didn't delete it. It existed, and so did I, parallel echoes, quiet and intact. I remember the memory tied to that message: the smell of the street outside their window, the sound of the ceiling fan whirring above, the way they leaned against the wall and laughed. That scene is gone, but it lingers in me, just as I linger in theirs, probably.

Sometimes, though, someone surprises you. A text out of the blue. A chance encounter. A laugh shared after months of silence. Those moments remind you that not all drift is absence. Some presences persist, threading through your days invisibly, shaping you even when unseen. The contrast between the soft exit and these lingering connections teaches you something essential: relationships are dynamic. They need attention, but they also survive your absence. And sometimes, that survival is its own kind of care.

Disappearing isn't about endings. It's about allowing continuity, of yourself, of others. You don't need closure. You don't need applause. You need distance. And with distance comes clarity: who you are when no one is watching, who they are when you aren't, and the quiet, unseen paths that intersect briefly before fading.

Perhaps that's the essence of a soft exit. Not erasure. Not avoidance. Just a gentle deceleration, a lowering of signal strength until your presence is felt only in the softest echoes. And in that silence, you finally see them, or yourself, as the spaces between light and shadow, the gaps where existence is felt, not announced.

patch notes

You aren't the person you were last year. Or last month. Or last week. Sometimes you notice it in the small things: a sharper joke when someone irritates you, a restraint that wasn't there before, a kindness extended without expectation. Other times, it's the absence, the temper you once wore like a badge, the certainty that's softened into a pause. Each moment of change is like a patch applied quietly, imperceptibly, sometimes without your permission.

When I was a kid, I dreamed in loud, unapologetic bursts: first an astronaut, then an author, then the Prime Minister of India. Each dream felt like a version of myself fully installed, ready to launch, ready to publish, ready to govern. Then life happened, or I happened, and some patches replaced those ambitions with subtler ones. I plan to major in computer science now, and it feels like another update: the essence of me is still intact, but the interface has changed.

I think about my old self when I scroll through childhood photos or videos. I cringe, sometimes, at my awkward smiles, the dramatic gestures, the vlogs I made on my old YouTube channel, little time capsules of an unpolished me. And yet, I laugh. I see the threads connecting that kid to the one who learns to let go of grudges, to move past what no longer serves me. Those patches weren't imposed; they were chosen, one at a time, sometimes painfully, sometimes unconsciously.

Updates arrive in unexpected forms. A friend corrects you, and you pause long enough to let the lesson sink in. A miscommunication with someone you love lingers in your mind, reshaping the way you phrase your next words. You adjust, recalibrate. Some patches are voluntary, some forced by circumstance. Some feel empowered. Others, like grudges or guilt, are installed against your will. And yet, letting go slowly becomes its own patch, a soft, self-applied update that frees memory space, emotional bandwidth, and your heart.

I notice how much of myself is borrowed, from friends, from those I've admired, from people I never realised I was imitating. A glance, a laugh, a mannerism, and suddenly you're different, a mosaic of all the people who have brushed against your life. You patch yourself with fragments of them, not because you want to be them, but because their presence leaves a subtle imprint on your reactions, your timing, your choices. Over time, these fragments accumulate, quietly rewriting your behaviours and your rhythms.

Some patches are sensory. I remember the exhilaration of holding someone's hand for the first time, the awkward hesitation before a hug you never got to give, the pang of realising you will never step into certain shared moments again. Other patches are emotional: the slow acceptance that people drift, that even your closest friend, once privy to your every pause, every joke, now exists largely in a parallel system you no longer operate within. No fallouts. No fights. Just silence. Just drift.

Patch notes are rarely shared. You don't announce every internal adjustment. Most of the time, they are invisible to everyone else, subtle shifts in tone, expression, or the way you pause before answering. But they matter to you. They shape how your system functions in the world, how you navigate relationships, and how you carry yourself in quiet moments.

One evening, I caught myself smiling at an old habit I'd abandoned. A part of me wanted to resurrect it, just for nostalgia's sake. But the new patch had already taken root. I didn't mourn the change. I admired it quietly. I realised survival often isn't about clinging to the old, but iterating responsibly, one small update at a time.

And in that, there's a subtle wisdom. You patch yourself not just to fix what's broken, but to anticipate what's coming. To navigate relationships without overloading your own system. To leave space for others to update themselves as well. To move through life with grace, knowing that who you were yesterday doesn't dictate who you must be today.

Perhaps the most important patch is learning how to let go. I was terrible at it once, holding grudges, wanting certain people entirely to myself, fearing their absence as though losing them meant losing a part of me. Slowly, I've begun to accept that everyone has intricate lives as complicated as my own, and that trying to hold someone in place only creates tension in both our systems. Drift is not abandonment; it's recognition that existence is multilayered, and that sometimes the most caring thing is to step back, to recede, to give someone their own bandwidth.

Maybe that's the quiet artistry of patch notes, the acknowledgement that you are never static, that continuity and change can coexist. Your evolution is ongoing, invisible, sometimes unnoticed, but profoundly shaping the way you experience the world. That kid who dreamed of space, or books, or governing a nation, they're still in there, layered beneath the updates, glimpsed when you scroll through old photos, smile at old vlogs, or feel your pulse quicken at a memory. Each patch isn't an erasure. Its growth.

the people you'll never be again

I often find myself face-to-face with the versions of me that no longer exist. Not just who I am today, but the selves I once inhabited: the fearless kid who ran barefoot through the street, the obsessive teenager who recorded every joke on a camera, the version who imagined being a prime minister or an astronaut. They're all still here, layered inside me, like snapshots in an archive, each with its own rhythm, each responding differently to the world.

I notice them in quiet moments. The version of me who laughed too loudly at a friend's story whispers from a memory; the one who overthought every gesture peers back through the hesitation in a pause. These versions coexist, invisible yet persistent, and sometimes they argue silently over decisions I make, over the way I act, over the people I allow into my life.

And then there are the others, the people who once filled entire afternoons, whose presence was a constant variable in my day. Friends who knew every inflexion in my voice, every half-formed thought, every pause in conversation. Now, they exist as flickers in my memory, or in notifications I scroll past with a detached thumb. No fights. No abrupt endings. Just the quiet acknowledgement that our timelines no longer intersect. I do not know how they go about their days anymore, what sunlight hits their windows in the morning, how they laugh when they are alone. The intimacy has transformed into fragments, and I am learning to hold those fragments lightly.

Sometimes, a sensory trace surprises me: a song that was once ours, a smell that recalls a street we walked, a glance at a photograph that reminds me of an afternoon I can't return to. For a moment, the past feels tangible, almost present, and I feel both joy and the strange ache of recognition. I realise that I am both observer and participant, watching my memories, feeling their weight, but unable to intervene.

I am learning that disappearance, both of others and of past versions of myself, is not failure. It is a soft intelligence. It is the mind accounting for the cost of attachment: which presences need tending, which can persist in absence, which layers of self can cohabitate without collapsing into tension. I used to fear losing people, clinging desperately, wanting them entirely to myself. Now, I see that letting go is not absence, but acknowledgement, a recognition that lives are intricate and self-contained, each layer complete in its own way.

Sometimes, memory surprises me in miniature flashes. I smile at a video I once recorded and cringe at my past self's exuberance, yet laugh at the same time. I see the child who imagined worlds far beyond my reach, the teenager who clung to grudges, the young adult who feared letting go. They are all fragments, stitched into the mosaic of who I am today. They are gone, yet permanent, shaping my choices, influencing how I move, colouring the ways I reach out, or refrain from reaching.

Contrast enters occasionally. A friend I haven't seen in years might message unexpectedly. A voice appears, a presence felt, not the same as before, but a gentle reminder of continuity. These moments are rare and sharp against the backdrop of drift. They remind me that while versions of ourselves vanish, memory is not empty. It is an active archive, a repository of emotion, experience, and identity. It carries both past attachments and the blueprints of resilience, teaching us how to move through the world with measured presence.

Ultimately, this chapter is about holding both absence and multiplicity gently. About recognising that the people you loved, the friends who were central, the selves you once inhabited, all exist in layered snapshots, some vivid, some faded. And through it, you learn to inhabit the present self with clarity: the self that remembers, that carries fragments without clutching, that accepts that not everything is held close, and that not every version must be repeated.

And in the quiet of these reflections, I find a kind of solace: that the versions of me and of others that no longer appear are not erased. They persist in memory, in subtle influence, in the mosaic of experience that shapes each new day. In letting go, I am not losing them. I am allowing the system to function, not perfectly, not permanently, but beautifully, with all its complexity and unpredictability.

nodes and networks

We are all nodes. Tiny points, pulsing quietly in a web far too vast to ever fully map. Some connections glow brightly: the friend who messages at odd hours, the laugh that lingers from a fleeting conversation, the glance in a crowded room that sticks without reason. Others fade, almost imperceptibly, faint as whispers along the edges of memory. And yet, every single interaction leaves its mark. Every shared laugh, every word exchanged, every gesture updates loops of who we are. Some reshape us entirely. Some barely touch the default settings.

I carry fragments of everyone I've known. Their laughter threads through my routines, their pauses echo in my thoughts. The weight of unspoken messages, the faint brush of hands in passing, the half-remembered look in a street window, all of it lingers. I leave fragments too, unseen, persistent, inevitable. We patch. We drift. We disappear. We return. Each memory is a variable. Each absence is a protocol quietly running in the background.

Sometimes noticing feels like reading an unfamiliar log written in code you don't fully understand. You feel someone's presence ripple through your world, a smile caught in a window reflection, a voice drifting across a corridor, and you realise that even when you step back, you are still part of the network, still leaving traces. You cannot know everything. You cannot control outcomes. But you can witness. You can care. You can act softly, acknowledging that the smallest gestures, the faintest attention, are sometimes enough.

Sonder is seeing the totality. Not the nodes themselves, not the obvious links, but the flow: countless lives humming beside yours, each running its own updates, its own private histories. Sometimes it appears most clearly in absence, a friend who once filled whole afternoons, a presence that fades into a quiet corner of your memory. You notice that even your absence leaves a trace, invisible yet persistent, shaping connections without demanding recognition.

The network continues, independent of your awareness. Connections spark, fade, and ripple outward. Attention, recognition, empathy, these are currencies measured not in applause but in awareness. And just as in an economy, where increasing rewards for production drives greater aggregate demand, in life, noticing, attending, and caring for others increases the vitality of the network around us.

And in noticing others, in leaving traces and receiving them, my own node evolves, updated, patched, reshaped by the quiet work of attention. Fragility and resilience coexist. We are compiling, updating, shifting, finite and infinite, fleeting and persistent. The pulse of lives intertwined carries on, whether you are aware of it or not.

reflections from the edge

You've already forgotten the first chapter. That's okay. So have I. Some people only exist in your browser history; you never meant to go back, but you haven't cleared it either. Maybe none of this is worth remembering. Maybe that's what makes it real.

I've written about drift, about patching, about the versions of ourselves we cannot inhabit again. I've written about the people we touch, the traces we leave, and the echoes that linger when attention moves on. I've written about seeing, really seeing, the infinite complexity of lives around us, some close, some distant, some only glimpsed in passing.

Connections are fragile, and yet they pulse quietly beneath the surface. A smile remembered, a message never sent, a pause that lingers longer than it should, each subtle action leaves an imprint. Just as in economics, when the reward for factors of production increases, aggregate demand rises, strengthening the entire system. In life, when we notice, attend, and care for the lives around us, the network hums more vividly; presence becomes a force of subtle vitality.

I carry fragments of everyone I've known. Their laughter in my routines, the way their pauses once shaped my timing, their habits etched into memory. And I leave fragments in them, unnoticed, persistent, gentle. Some traces glow like morning light; others hum cold, like a window left open at night. Some I'll revisit. Most I won't. And that is enough.

Sometimes I catch myself smiling at an old message I never sent. The screen glows in the dark room. My fingers hover over words I no longer need to write. I don't answer. I don't delete. It exists, and so do I, separate, quiet, unbroken. In these small moments, I feel the pulse of the network: the hum of lives intersecting, separating, overlapping. The energy of noticing, of caring, even softly, compounds, carrying forward in ways I cannot fully see.

And in all of this, my own node grows. I am updated by attention and absence, shaped by memory and lapse, and refined by fleeting moments of presence and care. Fragile and strong coexist. Finite and infinite, fleeting and persistent, threads in a system far larger than myself.

So I leave you here, at the edge of nodes, networks, fragments, and echoes. Let the pulse continue. Let it carry you. Notice. Remember. Drift. Patch. Reconnect. And in every small act of attention, touch the infinite.

Because, after all, it's not that deep… or is it?